IMAGES
of America
FORT MACON

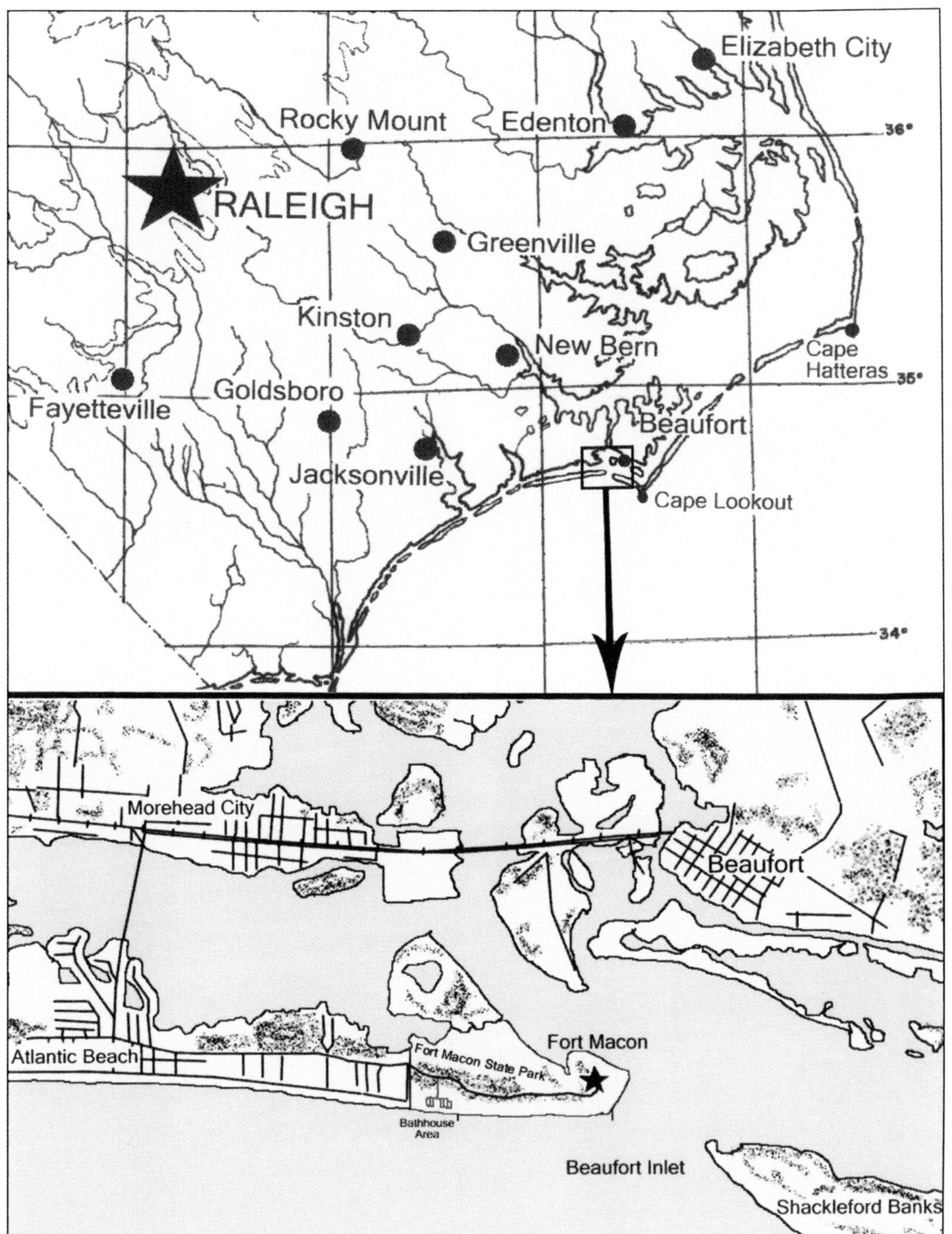

Map of the North Carolina Coast. This map of the North Carolina coast shows the location of Beaufort Harbor and the environs of Fort Macon. (Map by Kevin Bleck, Fort Macon State Park.)

On the Cover: Park visitors enjoy a view of the parade ground of Fort Macon in this publicity photograph taken for the North Carolina Department of Conservation and Development about the summer of 1940. (Fort Macon State Park archives.)

Paul R. Branch Jr.

ISBN 978-0-7385-9937-3

Published by Arcadia Publishing
Charleston, South Carolina

Printed in the United States of America

Library of Congress Control Number: 2012955616

For all general information, please contact Arcadia Publishing:
Telephone 843-853-2070
Fax 843-853-0044
E-mail sales@arcadiapublishing.com
For customer service and orders:
Toll-Free 1-888-313-2665

Visit us on the Internet at www.arcadiapublishing.com

Contents

ACKNOWLEDGMENTS

The bulk of the images in this work have come from the photographic archives of Fort Macon State Park, which consists of about 4,000 photographs and slides. These include images taken by the park staff over the years; publicity and documentary images taken by photographers of the North Carolina Department of Conservation and Development and Division of State Parks; and images donated by park visitors and military personnel. Also, some of the images related to the Civilian Conservation Corps work at Fort Macon are from Record Group 79, Records of the National Park Service, Entry 41, National Archives, College Park, Maryland (cited hereafter as National Park Service Records, National Archives). In addition to these, the author is grateful for images provided through the courtesy of the following: State Archives of North Carolina, Raleigh, ID No. 84.49, Department of Natural Resources and Community Development, Division of Forestry Resources Information and Education Photography (cited hereafter as Forestry Resources Collection, North Carolina State Archives); Bayard Morgan Wootten Photographic Collection (P0011), North Carolina Collection Photographic Archives, Wilson Library, University of North Carolina at Chapel Hill (cited hereafter as Bayard Wootten Photographic Collection, University of North Carolina); and the Casemate Museum, Fort Monroe, Virginia.

Thanks are also due to Bettie Woodson Weaver, Mallory Liles Jr., and former park superintendent Jody A. Merritt for contributing images for this work from their personal collections.

INTRODUCTION

Among the most prominent of the many historic attractions of coastal North Carolina is Fort Macon, situated on the eastern point of Bogue Banks in Carteret County. Fort Macon is a 19th-century masonry fortification that guards the entrance to Beaufort Harbor, one of North Carolina's two principal seaports. The fort is preserved today within Fort Macon State Park, the second oldest of North Carolina's state parks. Although quiet and peaceful now, the old fort's creation resulted from a time when, as a young country, the United States felt its maritime boundary was threatened by more powerful foreign nations.

In Colonial times, a succession of wars involving the New World colonies and the European powers of Spain, France, and Great Britain provided a constant threat of coastal raids by enemy warships. During these conflicts, the nearby town of Beaufort, North Carolina, the third-oldest town in the state, was captured and plundered by the Spanish in 1747. In the Revolutionary War, British warships were able to raid Beaufort Harbor in 1778 and 1782. Such attacks served to illustrate the need for the construction of fortifications on the eastern point of Bogue Banks that would be able to guard the harbor entrance against the incursion of enemy warships. An early effort to build a fort here in 1756 was unsuccessful, and the harbor remained defenseless during the remainder of the 18th century.

Following the Revolutionary War and through the early 19th century, the new United States experienced strained relations with both France and Great Britain. Fearing the threats posed to its security by these mighty European powers, two successive national defense systems of coastal fortifications were built by the United States to protect its maritime frontier against foreign aggression. As a part of these defenses, a small masonry fort named Fort Hampton was built on the eastern point of Bogue Banks during 1808–1809 to guard Beaufort Harbor. This fort protected the harbor during the subsequent War of 1812 but was abandoned shortly afterward. Shore erosion and a hurricane in 1825 were responsible for sweeping Fort Hampton into Beaufort Inlet.

The War of 1812 exposed the weakness of existing US coastal defenses against naval attack. As a result, the US government now began construction on a third improved system of coastal fortifications for national defense. This "Third System" ultimately called for the construction of a national defense chain of 38 new, permanent forts along the US coast. The construction of these forts began in 1817 and continued for more than five decades. The present Fort Macon was a part of this defense system.

Fort Macon was designed and built by the US Army Corps of Engineers between 1826 and 1834 on the eastern point of Bogue Banks overlooking the ship channel through Beaufort Inlet. Its namesake was North Carolina's eminent statesman of the period, Nathaniel Macon (1758–1837). The work required more than nine million bricks. The fort was built in the form of a pentagon with an outer defensive wall called the covertway and an inner main defensive citadel. Separating the two walls was a sunken area known as the ditch, which could be flooded with seawater and turned into a moat to provide an obstacle to an enemy attack. Inside the citadel were vaulted brick rooms called casemates, which served as living quarters, storerooms, and support facilities. Following its completion in December 1834, the fort was improved and modified between 1841 and 1846, including the installation of emplacements for 54 cannons. The total cost of the fort was $463,790.

As a result of Congressional economizing, the fort was used only intermittently over the years that followed. It was actively garrisoned only during the years of 1834–1836, 1842–1844, and 1848–1849. At other times, an ordnance sergeant acting as a caretaker was usually the only person stationed at the fort by the Army.

The War Between the States began on April 12, 1861. Two days later, local North Carolina militia forces from Beaufort and Morehead City seized Fort Macon from its Army caretaker for the State of North Carolina and the Confederacy. North Carolina Confederate forces then spent a year arming the fort with 54 heavy cannons and preparing it for battle. The fort's garrison ultimately consisted of five heavy artillery companies totaling more than 400 men commanded by Col. Moses J. White.

Early in 1862, Union major general Ambrose E. Burnside led a powerful amphibious expedition to capture strategic objectives in the eastern coastal region of North Carolina. After defeating Confederate forces at Roanoke Island and New Bern in February and March 1862, Burnside turned his attention to recapturing Fort Macon. The capture of the fort would allow both the Union army and navy to use Beaufort Harbor. Part of Burnside's command under Brig. Gen. John G. Parke was sent to capture Fort Macon in March and secure the use of the harbor. Advancing from New Bern, Parke's forces occupied Morehead City and Beaufort without resistance. An initial demand for the fort's surrender was offered on March 23, 1862. Col. Moses J. White and 402 North Carolina Confederates in the fort refused to surrender even though the fort was soon hopelessly outnumbered and surrounded.

Parke ferried his men, supplies, and siege artillery over to Bogue Banks and established three battery emplacements about three quarters of a mile from the fort for siege guns with which to bombard the fort into submission. Union infantry entrenched in the sand dunes nearby. Offshore, four Union navy gunboats blockaded the entrance to Beaufort Harbor and cooperated with Parke's land forces. Two other Union gunboats, one of them with General Burnside aboard, and two floating batteries took position in the sound northeast of the fort. The Confederates were completely surrounded, but they refused two final demands from General Burnside to surrender.

Just after dawn on April 25, 1862, Parke's forces opened fire on the fort with their heavy siege guns. They were aided for a time by the fire of the four Union navy gunboats in the ocean offshore and by one of the floating batteries in the sound to the northeast. The fort's guns easily repulsed the Union gunboat attack after only an hour and a half. However, the Confederates were unable to defend successfully against Parke's land batteries. Among Parke's siege guns was a battery of new rifled siege cannons, which were tremendously powerful and accurate at long range. These guns knocked out a number of the fort's cannons and were able to penetrate the fort's walls adjacent to the main gunpowder magazine. In all, the fort was hit 560 times by the three Union artillery batteries. Faced with extensive damage to the fort's walls and armament, and with one of the fort's magazines in danger of being exploded by the Union artillery fire, Colonel White had no choice but to raise the white flag over the fort at about 4:30 that afternoon. The bombardment ceased, and on the following morning, April 26, White formally surrendered the fort.

The Confederate garrison was paroled as prisoners of war. Despite the intensity of the bombardment, the fort's stout walls protected the garrison from suffering heavy losses. Seven Confederates were killed and 18 wounded. The Union losses were one killed and three wounded. The bombardment of Fort Macon was the second time in history that new, modern rifled siege cannons were used against a fort in combat. These powerful cannons demonstrated the growing obsolescence of masonry fortifications as a way of defense.

The Union army held Fort Macon for the remainder of the war. For part of the war, it was utilized not only for defense of the harbor but also as a military prison. Beaufort Harbor served as an important coaling and repair station for the Union navy during the war and as a staging area for other Union coastal operations.

During the Reconstruction Era, Fort Macon was continuously occupied as a US Army garrison post until 1877. Because there were no state or federal penitentiaries in the military district of North and South Carolina, Fort Macon was also used for about 11 years as a civil and military prison. The fort was deactivated in 1877, at the end of Reconstruction, and returned to caretaker status. However, during the summer of 1898, the fort was garrisoned once again for the Spanish-American War.

By the beginning of the 20th century, the US Army realized that Fort Macon and the other masonry coastal forts of its era were completely obsolete for modern defense. Accordingly, in December 1903, the fort was completely abandoned. In a very short time, vines, briars, and undergrowth choked its parade ground and ramparts. Its walls became almost hidden by a curtain of greenery. In the casemates, trim work decayed while plaster collapsed into heaps onto the rotten flooring below. Ironwork rusted away while doors swung useless in the wind. Even in this wild state, the fort was frequently visited by hunters, fishermen, curiosity seekers, and excursionists who had come by boat. Included among the latter were women and children who zealously tromped through the undergrowth with their parties to see its overgrown walls and dark, silent rooms.

During World War I, the fort was not occupied for defense. Following the end of that conflict, the US Army sought to dispense with its many old frontier posts and coastal forts that were no longer needed for national defense. Included among these was Fort Macon, which was placed on a list of surplus military properties in 1923 to be offered for sale by the Army. North Carolina government officials and the public recognized the historic importance of the old fort to the state and took steps to acquire it. North Carolina's Congressional leaders were able to have the fort and its surrounding reservation given to the State of North Carolina to be used as a public park for the sum of $1 by Congressional act on June 4, 1924. Fort Macon State Park became the second area, after Mount Mitchell, to be acquired by North Carolina as a state park.

Although Fort Macon was now a state park, there was no funding available to develop it. The park was placed under the state forestry division for management purposes. Forestry officials utilized the area around the fort for a number of years to plant pine seedlings and conduct experiments on which pine species were best adapted to the coastal environment. Visitors continued their excursions to see the fort by boat until a bridge was constructed from the mainland to Bogue Banks in 1928. Thereafter, they were able to drive down the beach by automobile to visit the fort. The state forestry division hired a part-time warden to be on hand at the fort several days a week as funding allowed.

The Great Depression gave North Carolina the opportunity to finally develop its parks for the public through the Civilian Conservation Corps (CCC). The CCC was a federal work relief program that provided jobs for unemployed young men to work on public conservation and natural resource projects. A CCC camp was stationed at Fort Macon in April 1934 and worked in the park until October 1935. The CCC workers cleared out the jungle growing inside the fort and partly restored some of its rooms. They completed a public road to the park from the town of Atlantic Beach and built public recreational facilities such as a picnic shelter, rest rooms, a vacation cabin, a parking lot, and a house for the caretaker. Following the completion of their work, Fort Macon State Park officially opened to the public on May 1, 1936, as North Carolina's first functioning state park.

Over the next several years, increasing numbers of visitors came to enjoy the park. The state made plans to expand the park's facilities to include a beach recreation area with the assistance of another federal work relief program called the Works Progress Administration (WPA). Under the WPA, construction began in 1940 on a bathhouse, concession stand, boardwalk, and parking lot. Unfortunately, work stopped before the facilities were completed due to the approach of World War II.

With the entry of the United States into World War II in December 1941, the US Army recognized the need to occupy the fort again to protect a number of important nearby facilities.

Army Coast Artillery troops arrived to actively occupy the fort again for the war emergency. Soldiers lived in the fort and in barracks erected just outside. Harbor defense headquarters were also established in the fort. Shore batteries were established on the beach just outside the fort to guard against coastal raids by German submarines. Although these defenses were never called upon to fight the enemy, their presence served as a deterrent that forced the German U-boats to keep their distance. The Army occupied the fort and park from December 1941 to November 1944 under a special lease arrangement with the State of North Carolina. At the end of the war, the troops and weaponry were withdrawn. On October 1, 1946, the Army returned Fort Macon State Park to the state.

After the war, much work was required to undo the effects of Army occupation to make the fort presentable to the public again. The bathhouse recreational facilities were finally opened for the first time in 1949. During the 1950s and 1960s, there was much development of the park's facilities. This included a museum in the fort, expansion of the parking lots, new rest rooms, a picnic shelter, barracks for summer personnel, maintenance facilities, houses for the park staff, a park office, and a modern bathhouse. Since that time, there have been additional improvements made over the years, such as the restoration and renovation of the fort and the addition of a modern visitor center.

The park's visitation has increased steadily over the years, so that today, Fort Macon State Park is one of the most visited state parks in North Carolina. It has more than a million visitors each year. Thus from a lonely military post in the early 19th century, Fort Macon has evolved into a beloved state park where its rich history is preserved as a remembrance to another time and place in our country's history. The park today offers a unique blend of history, nature, and recreational opportunities to the public and is truly one of the wonders of coastal North Carolina.

One

Fort Macon as a 19th-Century Military Post

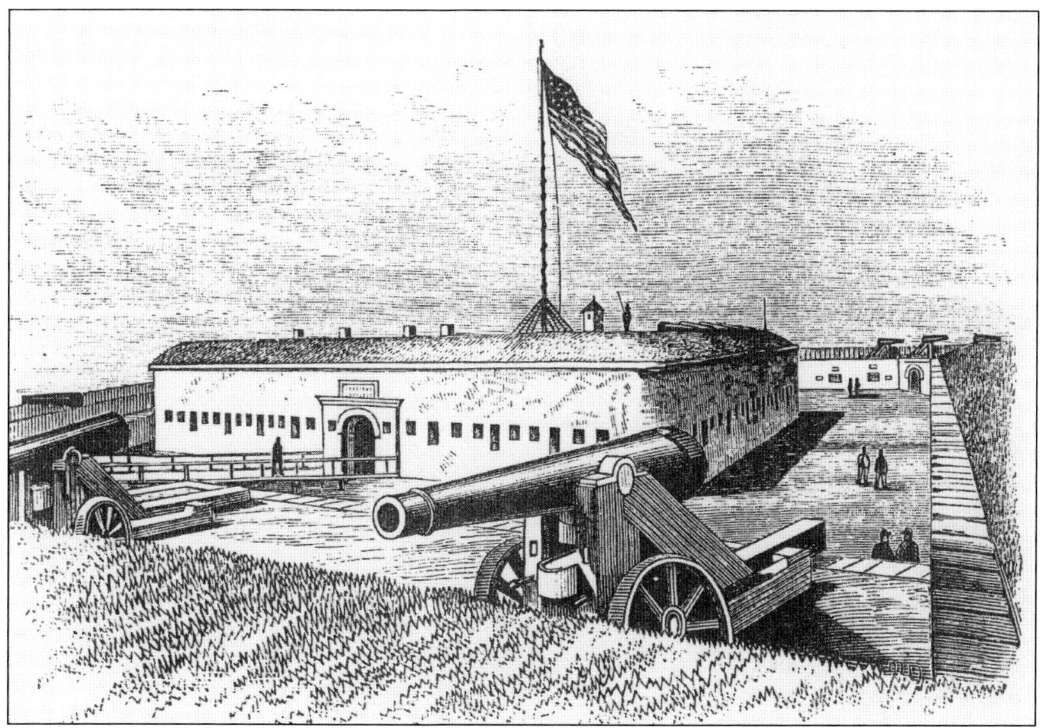

Fort Macon, c. 1864. This woodcut drawing shows the main entrance, or sally port, of Fort Macon in 1864 during the War Between the States. (Fort Macon State Park archives.)

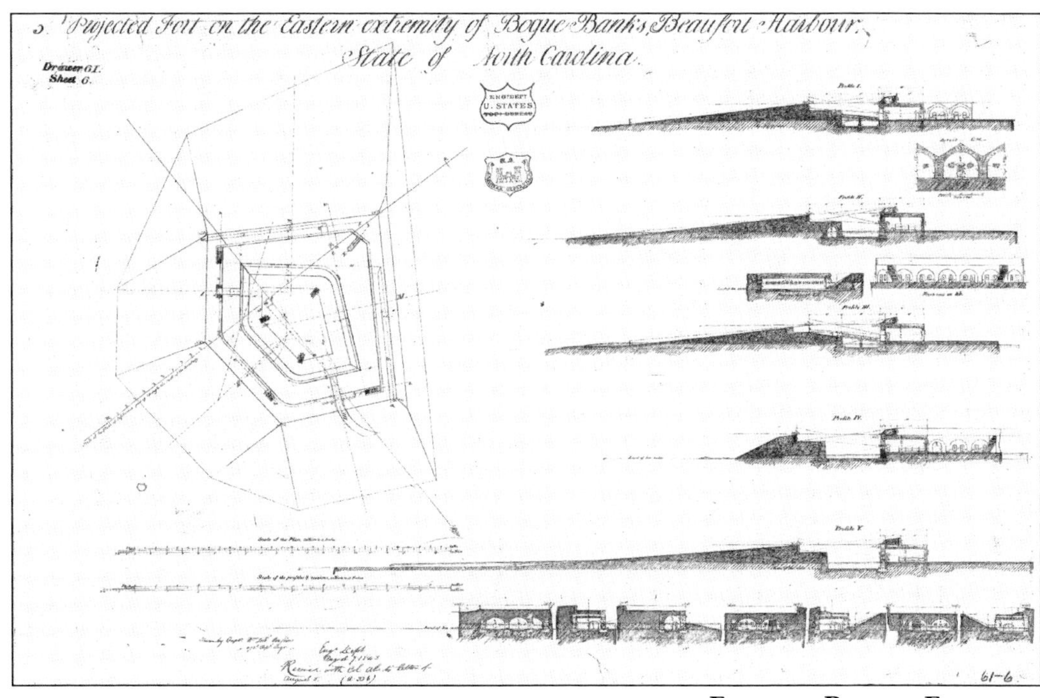

Engineer Plan of Fort Macon, 1821. This engineer plan of Fort Macon was drafted for the US Army Corps of Engineers in 1821 by Capt. William Tell Poussin, cartographer to Brig. Gen. Simon Bernard, the architect of Fort Macon. It shows the plan of the fort with section profiles. (Cartographic and Architectural Section, National Archives.)

Nathaniel Macon. The namesake of Fort Macon, Nathaniel Macon (1758–1837), was North Carolina's eminent statesman and a national political figure in the early decades of the country's history. He served for decades in both houses of the US Congress and was active in state and national politics for most of his adult life. (North Carolina State Archives.)

FORT MACON'S LAYOUT. Fort Macon has an outer defensive wall (the covertway) and a main inner defense (the citadel), separated by a sunken ditch, which could be flooded with seawater for defense. Rooms under the covertway at locations marked C are counterfire galleries for flanking defense. The citadel has a main entrance (sally port) and a rear entrance (postern). The sloped earth glacis surrounds the fort. (Fort Macon State Park archives.)

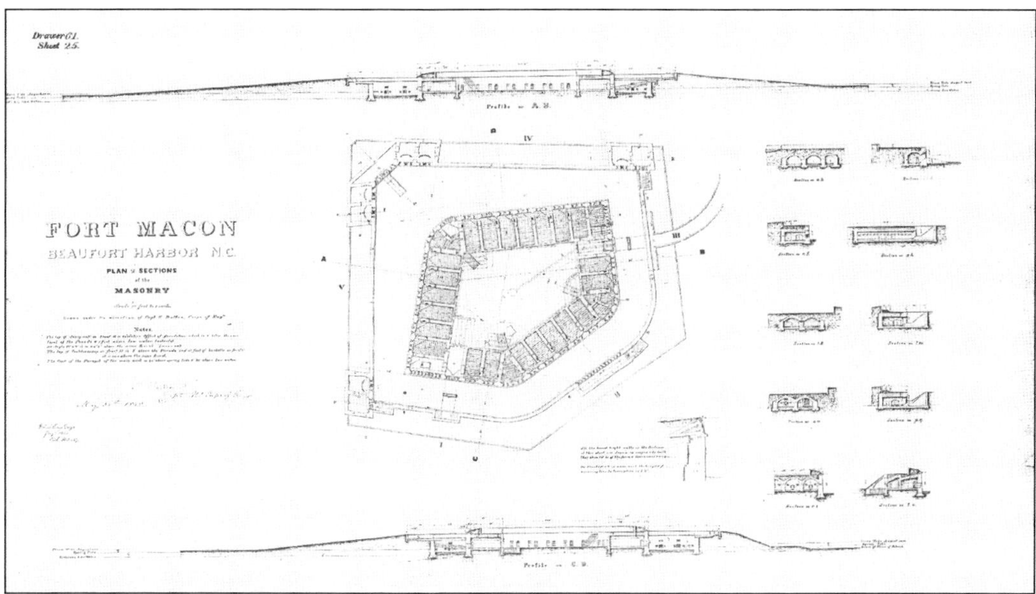

FORT MACON ENGINEER PLANS AND SECTIONS. This 1842 engineering drawing shows plans and sections of Fort Macon. The rooms in the central citadel are called casemates and provided soldiers with living and working quarters. Most of the casemates had wood floors, plaster-finished walls, doors, windows, and trim. The four sets of counterfire galleries are shown under the covertway. (Cartographic and Architectural Section, National Archives.)

UNION SOLDIERS ENTRENCHED OUTSIDE FORT MACON, 1862. After 27 years of irregular use as an Army garrison post, Fort Macon was seized by North Carolina Confederate soldiers on April 14, 1861, at the beginning of the War Between the States. In March and April 1862, Union forces besieged the fort and its Confederate garrison. Here, Union observers (foreground) watch the fort (background center) from their entrenchments. (Fort Macon State Park archives.)

UNION 10-INCH MORTAR BATTERY. On April 25, 1862, Union forces opened fire on Fort Macon with a battery of four 10-inch siege mortars, a battery of four 8-inch siege mortars, and a battery of three 30-pounder Parrott rifled cannons. This sketch shows the 10-inch mortar battery in action that morning. The battery was commanded by Lt. Daniel W. Flagler. (Fort Macon State Park archives.)

Union Parrott Rifle Battery. This sketch shows the battery of three 30-pounder Parrott rifles in action against the fort on April 25, 1862. Commanded by Capt. Lewis O. Morris, these rifled cannons were very destructive, knocking out some of the fort's guns, penetrating the fort's walls, and threatening to detonate the fort's gunpowder magazines. (Fort Macon State Park archives.)

Union Naval Squadron. During the bombardment of Fort Macon, a squadron of four Union navy gunboats engaged the fort from the ocean (from left to right, *State of Georgia*, *Daylight*, *Chippewa*, and *Gemsbok*). Two of the gunboats were damaged by the fort's fire, and the squadron withdrew from the battle after only an hour and a half. (Fort Macon State Park archives.)

THE BOMBARDMENT OF FORT MACON, APRIL 25, 1862. This romanticized sketch shows the three Union artillery batteries (foreground) and Union navy gunboats bombarding Fort Macon

(background with flag) on April 25, 1862. After 11 hours of pounding from the Union land batteries, the fort was badly damaged and forced to surrender. (Fort Macon State Park archives.)

5TH RHODE ISLAND BATTALION ENTERING FORT MACON. On the morning of April 26, 1862, Union soldiers of the 5th Rhode Island Battalion marched up to formally receive the surrender of Fort Macon. Here, the column of Rhode Islanders marches up the fort glacis and circles around the top of the outer wall. (Fort Macon State Park archives.)

SURRENDER OF FORT MACON, APRIL 26, 1862. This sketch shows the Confederate garrison of Fort Macon preparing to depart as prisoners on the morning of the fort's surrender. A detachment of Union soldiers pulls down the Confederate flag. The Confederates were paroled and transported back to their own lines to await exchange. (Fort Macon State Park archives.)

West Wall after the Battle. This sketch made after the battle shows the damage done by Union artillery to the west wall of Fort Macon. After taking possession of the fort, Union soldiers repaired the damage and bricked up the holes in the walls made by the artillery fire. (*Battles and Leaders of the Civil War*, vol. I. New York: Century, 1887.)

Fort Ramparts after the Battle. This sketch shows the ramparts and parade ground of the fort after the battle. Union officers counted 560 actual hits on the fort by their artillery fire. (*Battles and Leaders of the Civil War*, vol. I. New York: Century, 1887.)

FORT MACON, JANUARY 7, 1863. While stationed at Fort Macon, Union corporal James W. Champney of the 45th Massachusetts Regiment made this sketch looking along the supply railroad leading from the wharf to the fort. (North Carolina State Archives.)

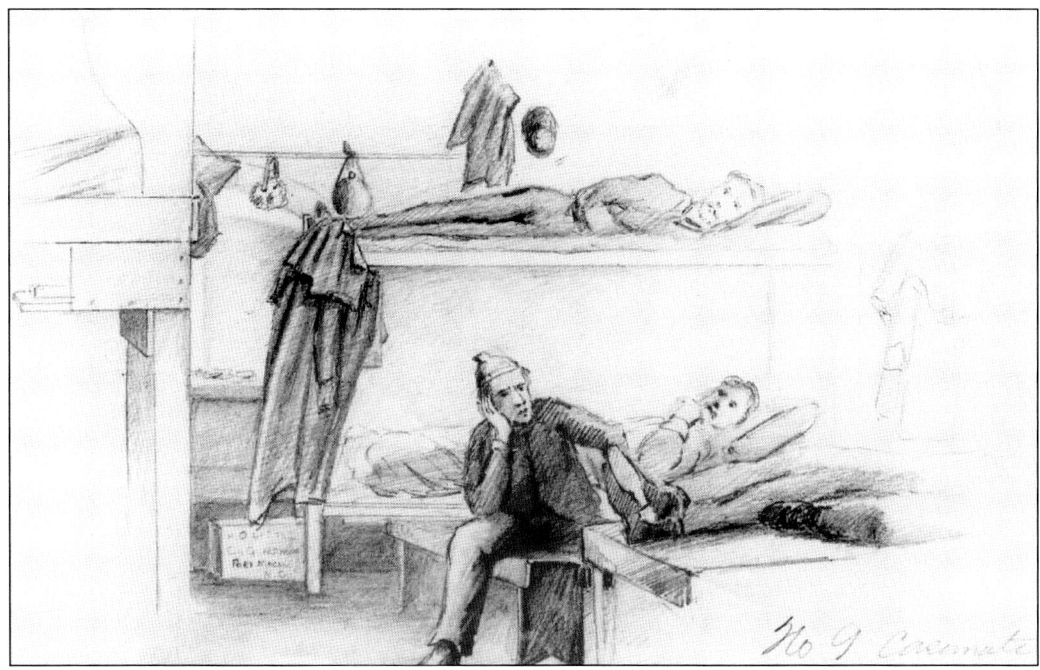

INTERIOR OF CASEMATE 9. Another Champney sketch shows the soldier barracks in Casemate 9 of Fort Macon in 1863. Soldiers normally slept on four-man wooden bunks with 20 to 40 men to a casemate. (North Carolina State Archives.)

SALLY PORT ENTRANCE, 1867. The only known photographs of Fort Macon in the 19th century were taken after the War Between the States in 1867. This one shows a group of two officers, three women, and a child on the sally port bridge. (Fort Macon State Park archives.)

SALLY PORT BRIDGE, 1867. This photograph shows a group of officers lounging on the sally port bridge and a sentry on guard at support arms. (Fort Macon State Park archives.)

Postern Bridge, 1867. This photograph shows another sentry standing guard at the postern bridge, with three of the fort's largest cannons in the background. The roofs of officers' quarters are visible at the left. (Fort Macon State Park archives.)

Southwest Front, 1867. This photograph looks along the southwest front toward the three cannons in the previous photograph. Note the piles of cannonballs stacked along the wall. (Fort Macon State Park archives.)

East Side of the Parade Ground, 1867. This view looks toward the casemates of the eastern fronts of the fort. The five casemates between the two stairs were officers' quarters. (Fort Macon State Park archives.)

Rifled 32-pounders, 1867. Two rifled 32-pounder cannons stand in the foreground of this photograph. A 100-pounder Parrott rifle is in the background. Only a handful of the more than 50 cannons that were once in the fort remained at the time this photograph was taken. (Fort Macon State Park archives.)

West Side of the Parade Ground, 1867. This photograph shows the casemates of the western fronts of the fort. The casemates on the right are prison casemates and serve as the quarters for prisoners held in the fort. Some of the prisoners are visible in the windows and doorways watching soldiers drilling in the parade ground. (Fort Macon State Park archives.)

SUPPLY RAILROAD, 1867. This photograph looks along the supply railroad leading from the wharf to the fort. Supplies were off-loaded at the wharf onto flatcars pulled by horses or mules to the fort. Note the large stack of firewood to the left. (Fort Macon State Park archives.)

OFFICER'S COTTAGE, 1867. Some of the fort's senior officers were housed in small cottages outside the fort. This is one of several that sat around the fort. In 1869, new officers' quarters were erected along the northeast glacis, leaving these older cottages for use by laundresses. (Fort Macon State Park archives.)

Two

Fort Macon Abandoned

Sally Port Entrance, c. 1910. Fort Macon was formally abandoned by the Army in 1903 in the belief that it would never be needed for war again. For more than three decades, it sat deserted. In this photograph, the wooden structure on top of the fort is a benchmark reference marker for the US Coast and Geodetic Survey. (Cartographic and Architectural Section, National Archives.)

Roadway into the Fort, c. 1924. The old brick and cobblestone roadway into the fort is mostly gone in this photograph. Note that the geodetic survey marker has changed. (Fort Macon State Park archives.)

Sally Port Entrance Looking from the North Angle, c. 1924. In this photograph, notice that the bridge has collapsed into ruins. (Fort Macon State Park archives.)

Postern Entrance Looking from the South Angle, c. 1924. The bridge at the postern entrance to the fort has also collapsed. (Fort Macon State Park archives.)

Closer View of the Postern Entrance, c. 1924. In this photograph, someone has erected a wooden walkway to gain access into the fort. (Fort Macon State Park archives.)

SOUTHWEST DITCH, C. 1924. This view looks along the weed-choked southwest avenue of the ditch from the south angle of the covertway. The gun ports of the southwest counterfire gallery are visible in the distance. (Fort Macon State Park archives.)

SOUTHWEST DITCH, EARLY 1900S. This view looks back along the southwest avenue of the ditch toward the south angle of the covertway. The mound of earth visible at the right is a traverse mound erected in 1898 to shield two 10-inch mortars mounted on the covertway from enemy gunfire during an attack. (Bayard Wootten Photographic Collection, University of North Carolina.)

NORTHWEST DITCH, EARLY 1900S. This photograph looks along the northwest ditch from the southwest angle of the covertway. (Fort Macon State Park archives.)

SALLY PORT INTERIOR, C. 1924. This view shows the interior of the sally port looking out through the main gates. Note that many of the wood blocks of the floor are missing. (Fort Macon State Park archives.)

Sally Port Interior, Early 1900s. This view looks through the sally port into the parade ground. The two large gates lie on the floor because vandals tore off their bronze hinges and sold them. Vandals also broke out windows, scrawled graffiti, and carried off anything of value they could find. (Bayard Wootten Photographic Collection, University of North Carolina.)

Parade Ground from the Sally Port, Early 1900s. This is a closer view that looks into the overgrown parade ground from the sally port. (Bayard Wootten Photographic Collection, University of North Carolina.)

Northeast Stairs, c. 1924. In this winter view, the northeast stairs are overgrown with vines and briars. (Fort Macon State Park archives.)

Northeast Stairs and Sally Port, c. 1924. This winter view from the parade ground looks back toward the overgrown northeast stairs and sally port. (Fort Macon State Park archives.)

NORTHEAST STAIRS, EARLY 1900S. This photograph of the northeast stairs was taken in the spring or summer, when the foliage of the vines and briars was full. (Fort Macon State Park archives.)

SOUTHEAST STAIRS, EARLY 1900S. This photograph looks along the east front of the parade ground toward the overgrown southeast stairs. (Bayard Wootten Photographic Collection, University of North Carolina.)

Southeast Stairs, c. 1920s. Judging from how much the undergrowth and vines have grown, this photograph was taken a few years after the preceding photograph. (North Carolina 5s.)

East Front from the Ramparts, Early 1900s. This photograph was taken shortly after the fort was abandoned, judging by how little the vegetation has grown. Rotten doors, windows, and woodwork can be seen lying among the undergrowth. (North Carolina State Archives.)

East Front, c. 1924. These overgrown casemates are officers' quarters on the east front of the parade ground. (Fort Macon State Park archives.)

Casemate 7, Early 1900s. This is a close view of the front of Casemate 7 on the east front of the parade ground. Part of its window still hangs in place. (Bayard Wootten Photographic Collection, University of North Carolina.)

SOUTHEAST FRONT, c. 1924. This view from an old lantern slide shows the overgrown southeast front of the parade ground. (Fort Macon State Park archives.)

EAST FRONT LOOKING FROM THE SOUTHEAST STAIRS, EARLY 1900s. This photograph looks along the east front of the parade ground toward the northeast stairs with full summer foliage. (Fort Macon State Park archives.)

NORTHWEST FRONT, C. 1909. This early photograph looks along the northwest front of the parade ground from near the sally port. Trees have already begun to grow in the parade ground. (North Carolina State Archives.)

NORTHWEST FRONT FROM THE RAMPARTS, EARLY 1900S. This view looks across the parade ground toward the southwest stairs and northwest front. (Bayard Wootten Photographic Collection, University of North Carolina.)

SOUTHEAST FRONT FROM THE RAMPARTS, EARLY 1920S. This view looks across the parade ground toward the southeast front and southeast stairs. (Forestry Resources Collection, North Carolina State Archives.)

SOUTHEAST STAIRS AND MAGAZINE DOOR, EARLY 1900S. In this photograph, the outer door to the southeast magazine lies on the southeast stairs after vandals ripped the bronze hinges off the door. (William Graham Collection, Fort Macon State Park archives.)

Southeast Angle and Parade Ground from the Ramparts, Early 1900s. This view looks across the parade ground from the ramparts toward the same stairs in the preceding photograph. (William Graham Collection, Fort Macon State Park archives.)

The Parade Ground from the Ramparts, Early 1900s. This is a similar view to the preceding photograph looking across the overgrown parade ground. (William Graham Collection, Fort Macon State Park archives.)

INTERIOR OF CASEMATE 8, c. 1924. This damaged photograph shows the interior of Casemate 8, with the plaster walls falling down and the interior woodwork rotting away. Note the graffiti left by visitors. (Fort Macon State Park archives.)

MAGAZINE ENTRANCE, c. 1924. This view shows the entrance to the southeast magazine in Casemate 8. The magazine's interior door lies propped against the entrance after vandals tore off its bronze hinges. Note the piles of lath strips and plaster that have collapsed into the floor from the furring above. (Fort Macon State Park archives.)

Early Visitors at the Sally Port Bridge, 1907. Thomas C. Woodson snapped this picture of his new bride, Bettie Winfree Woodson (center), and two other unidentified people in front of the sally port on June 28, 1907, during their honeymoon. The rotting sally port bridge had not yet collapsed. (Bettie Woodson Weaver, Midlothian, Virginia.)

Early Visitors in Fort Macon, c. 1909. This photograph shows an early group of visitors to Fort Macon in 1909. They are, from left to right, Mary Hendren, Caroline Hendren Roberts of New Bern, Dr. L.L. Hendren, Dr. Powell Stephens, Mabel Chadwick, Carolyn Cobb, Lucy Stanton, and unidentified. They are very nicely dressed for an excursion to an overgrown, abandoned fort. The next two photographs show women from this same group. (North Carolina State Archives.)

Woman at the Window, c. 1909. This photograph shows a pensive Caroline Hendren Roberts standing at the window of Casemate 7 in 1909. (North Carolina State Archives.)

Woman in the Magazine, c. 1909. Carolyn Cobb emerges from the southeast magazine in 1909. Compare this photograph of the magazine entrance to that on page 41. (North Carolina State Archives.)

VISITORS IN FORT MACON, EARLY 1900s. This photograph shows another group of excursionists exploring Fort Macon. (Lloyd Staton Collection, Fort Macon State Park archives.)

VISITOR GROUP, EARLY 1900s. The same group as in the preceding photograph poses on the northeast stairs. (Lloyd Staton Collection, Fort Macon State Park archives.)

VISITOR IN THE PARADE GROUND, EARLY 1920S. A visitor walks through the overgrown parade ground past the southwest stairs. Is he scratching the mosquito bites on his left arm? (Fort Macon State Park archives.)

VISITOR ON THE STAIRS, EARLY 1920S. Here, a visitor poses on the southeast stairs in the early 1920s. Note the section of bricks in the middle of the third step from the bottom. The step was damaged by artillery fire during the 1862 battle and was repaired with bricks by the Union army. (Lucy Benjamin Collection, Fort Macon State Park archives.)

VISITORS IN THE PARADE GROUND, EARLY 1900S. Two men survey the overgrown parade ground in this damaged photograph. (Bayard Wootten Photographic Collection, University of North Carolina.)

EXTERIOR OF FORT MACON, C. 1924. Unlike the jungle growing inside the fort, the exterior slopes and grounds around the fort were clear and open. In this view from the watchtower of the adjacent Coast Guard station, notice the cattle grazing on the slopes of the fort. (Fort Macon State Park archives.)

LIVESTOCK ON THE SLOPES, EARLY 1900s. This scene looks south toward the ocean with cattle grazing on the glacis of the fort. (William Graham Collection, Fort Macon State Park archives.)

VIEW NORTH OF THE FORT, 1927. This view shows marshlands and a savannah-like area extending northward from the fort. The building in the distance is a hunting cabin known as the Nicoll Cottage. (Forestry Resources Collection, North Carolina State Archives.)

View Northeast of the Fort, 1934. This view looks farther to the right of the previous photograph and shows more of the same open ground around Fort Macon. The brick structure to the right is a cistern that originally served one of the officers' quarters that stood outside the fort. The officers' quarters were long gone when this photograph was made, but the cistern still remains to this day. (Forestry Resources Collection, North Carolina State Archives.)

Forestry Worker Planting Trees, February 4, 1927. After Fort Macon became a state park in 1924, it was managed for many years by the North Carolina Division of Forestry. Forestry workers took advantage of the open grounds around the deserted fort to plant pine tree seedlings to determine which species survived best in the coastal environment of the Outer Banks. This worker uses a sack to illuminate a tiny seedling for the camera. (Forestry Resources Collection, North Carolina State Archives.)

Forestry Worker with Pine Tree, December 13, 1927. Forestry worker Addie Pace uses a box to illuminate a young pine tree planted the previous February for the camera. Pace and another worker planted 3,250 more seedlings on December 12 and 13, 1927. (Forestry Resources Collection, North Carolina State Archives.)

Forestry Worker Planting Seedlings. In the grassy area around the fort, a forestry worker uses a spade to make a hole to plant a seedling. The work of planting the thousands of seedlings around the fort in this manner was undoubtedly very monotonous and time-consuming for the workers. (Forestry Resources Collection, North Carolina State Archives.)

Surveying Their Work, April 9, 1931. Forestry worker W.J. Clark surveys the progress of young pine trees planted on the south glacis of Fort Macon in 1927. Visible in the background is the US Coast Guard station established in 1904 to the west of the old fort. (Forestry Resources Collection, North Carolina State Archives.)

Aftermath of a Fire, August 10, 1932. On August 3, 1932, a group of young park visitors accidentally started a fire in the grass on the fort glacis. The fire swept out of control through the grasslands and pine plantations around the fort and surrounding area. It wiped out in one afternoon all the years of work and experimentation by the forestry division with planting and growing pine trees for the coast. The hundreds of scorched pine trees planted by the forestry division were wiped out, as this photograph shows. (Forestry Resources Collection, North Carolina State Archives.)

FORT MACON'S COVERTWAY, AUGUST 10, 1932. The fire of August 3, 1932, also swept through the vegetation on the fort's outer wall and glacis. However, it did not spread to the fort's interior or to the adjacent Coast Guard station. (Forestry Resources Collection, North Carolina State Archives.)

Beach Stabilization, April 9, 1931. In addition to planting pine trees around the fort, forestry workers also realized the unstable nature of the ocean beach adjacent to the fort. They planted rows of beach grass to aid the formation of sand dunes to help stabilize the beach and prevent erosion. (Forestry Resources Collection, North Carolina State Archives.)

Cannonball on the Beach, July 29, 1930. As forestry workers went about their activities during these early years of Fort Macon State Park's existence, they were occasionally reminded of the fort's history and purpose. Here a worker points to a 32-pounder cannonball from the fort lying uncovered on the beach. (Forestry Resources Collection, North Carolina State Archives.)

Three

A Functioning Park

Surveying His Work, 1935. A Civilian Conservation Corps (CCC) worker inspects his work during the restoration of Fort Macon. From April 1934 to October 1935, a Civilian Conservation Corps camp worked at Fort Macon State Park to clear out and restore the old fort, build a road to the park, and establish park facilities for the public. The park then operated from its official opening in 1936 until the advent of World War II. (Fort Macon State Park archives.)

CCC Temporary Camp. This photograph was taken in April 1934 after Civilian Conservation Corps Company 432 arrived to begin work in Fort Macon State Park. The workers were first housed in a tent camp outside the fort. (Forestry Resources Collection, North Carolina State Archives.)

Clearing out the Fort. One of the first jobs facing the CCC workers was to clear out the jungle of vines, briars, and bushes growing inside the fort. In this photograph, they have already made great progress in this task. (National Park Service Records, National Archives.)

Clearing the Parade Ground. In this photograph, the CCC workers have cut down and cleared out most of the heavy vegetation in the parade ground of the fort. However, the larger trees were left and would remain for years. (Fort Macon State Park archives.)

The Parade Ground Looking North. This view from the ramparts above looks down into the parade ground as CCC workers perform various tasks. In addition to clearing out the vegetation, these tasks included relaying the brick sidewalks around the parade ground, cleaning out the casemates, and restoring one half of the fort with windows, doors, and trim work. (Fort Macon State Park archives.)

The Parade Looking Northeast. In this view, the sidewalks along the east front have been relaid and rotten windows and doors removed. The large mound of earth on the rampart at the right is a remnant of a traverse mound erected during the Spanish-American War in 1898 to shield a 100-pounder Parrott rifle cannon from possible enemy fire. (Fort Macon State Park archives.)

CCC Workers in the Parade Ground. This photograph shows CCC workers cutting bricks for the sidewalk near the sally port entrance. Note the man on the ladder at the left trimming dead limbs out of the cedar tree. (Fort Macon State Park archives.)

Removing the Traverse Mound. Workers are engaged here in removing the Spanish-American War traverse mound on the ramparts of the east front of the fort. Although the mound was historic, the CCC wished to return the fort to its appearance earlier in the 19th century. (Fort Macon State Park archives.)

Looking into the Parade Ground from the Ramparts. In this view, much of the work clearing the parade ground and laying sidewalks appears to have been finished. Notice that the Spanish-American War traverse mound is now gone at the right. (Fort Macon State Park archives.)

Looking along the East Front. This photograph shows the casemates along the east front of the parade ground cleaned out and ready to be restored. The CCC workers would restore the nine casemate fronts on the eastern half of the parade ground to their original appearance by installing replica windows, shutters, doors, and wood trim. (Fort Macon State Park archives.)

Laying Brick Sidewalks. Here several workers are relaying the sidewalk along the southwest front of the parade ground. The sidewalks extended all around the five fronts of the parade ground. Workers reused the original bricks when possible. (Fort Macon State Park archives.)

SIDEWALKS ON THE SOUTHWEST FRONT. This view of the men in the preceding photograph shows the progress they have made in restoring the sidewalk along the southwest front of the parade ground. The circular object in the foreground is a hatch leading to a water cistern located under the walkway. (Fort Macon State Park archives.)

SIDEWALKS ON THE NORTHWEST FRONT. This view shows workers relaying the sidewalks along the northwest front of the fort. The sally port entrance is in the background. (Fort Macon State Park archives.)

Roadway to the Sally Port. CCC workers are busy in this photograph restoring the brick and cobblestone roadway leading to the sally port bridge. Two bands of cobblestones were originally set into the roadway spaced the width of an average wagon to better withstand the wear of wagon wheels. Other men are making repairs to the adjacent wing-wall. (National Park Service Records, National Archives.)

Rebuilding the Sally Port Bridge. Workmen rebuild the bridge across the ditch to the sally port. The original bridges here and at the postern entrance had long since rotted away and collapsed. Neither of the original bridges were drawbridges that could be raised to stop intruders. (National Park Service Records, National Archives.)

Sally Port Bridge. In this photograph, the planking of the new sally port bridge is almost complete. New railings would complete the bridge. (National Park Service Records, National Archives.)

Completed Postern Bridge. This photograph shows the postern bridge as completed. The sally port bridge had the same appearance once finished. (National Park Service Records, National Archives.)

Restored East Front. This photograph shows the casemates of the east front of the parade ground restored. Replica windows, shutters, and doors have been installed, and a workman is busy painting the trim work. (Fort Macon State Park archives.)

Applying Finishing Touches to Casemate 7. This photograph of the interior of Casemate 7 shows a workman painting the door trim. With its new wood floor, windows, door, shutters, and trim work, the casemate is complete. (National Park Service Records, National Archives.)

Waterproofing the Casemates. The CCC workers found that many of the casemates leaked during rain. To prevent this, it was necessary to dig out sections of earth over the casemates and make repairs. This photograph shows a workman in an excavated section at the south angle of the rampart. (National Park Service Records, National Archives.)

Waterproofing Repairs. The photograph shows a workman nestled between excavated sections over the casemates making masonry repairs. (Fort Macon State Park archives.)

Workmen Waterproofing Casemates 5 and 6. When CCC workers excavated over the casemates, they found that the leaks were frequently caused by cracks that allowed water to enter where the casemate arches met the parade wall. These men are filling the cracks with grout to stop the leaking. The bulge in the wall was caused by a Union cannon shot during the bombardment of Fort Macon in 1862. (Fort Macon State Park archives.)

CCC Camp Dobbs. While some of the CCC workers labored in Fort Macon, others were engaged in establishing a permanent camp for the men of Company 432. This sprawling camp, known as Camp Dobbs, was established near the beach southwest of the fort. Prefabricated military buildings were used as barracks, offices, storerooms, and a mess hall. The camp was completed in September 1934. (Fort Macon State Park archives.)

Closer View of Camp Dobbs Buildings. In this photograph, a garage building is visible at the right, and barracks for the workers are at the left. The building in the rear is the mess hall and kitchen. (Forestry Resources Collections, North Carolina State Archives.)

Another View of Camp Dobbs Buildings. This photograph shows the garage (left), tool house and shop (center), and office (right). The mess hall is in the left background. (Forestry Resources Collections, North Carolina State Archives.)

Camp Barracks and Mess Hall. This photograph shows a row of barracks at the left and the end of the mess hall at the right. The camp buildings were "demountable" buildings furnished by the US Army. They could be taken apart and reassembled elsewhere as CCC companies moved on to different projects. (Forestry Resources Collections, North Carolina State Archives.)

The Road from Atlantic Beach. A major project of the CCC workers was to complete a nearly four-mile stretch of clay road between the town of Atlantic Beach and Fort Macon. In late 1933, a federal work project under the Civil Works Administration had begun building the road, but it was never completed. In this photograph from January 20, 1934, state engineers stand at the point where the road construction stopped. (Forestry Resources Collection, North Carolina State Archives.)

Unfinished Road Looking East, January 20, 1934. Here a state engineer stands at the point where road construction stopped. The view looks east toward Fort Macon State Park and shows that the roadbed has been cleared for part of the way ahead but nothing more. (Forestry Resources Collection, North Carolina State Archives.)

Loading Clay for the Road, September 1934. During their time at Fort Macon State Park, some of the CCC workers were sent to complete the unfinished road from Atlantic Beach. In this photograph, CCC workers are loading clay into dump trucks to be hauled to the point where other workers are building the road. (National Park Service Records, National Archives.)

Road Surfacing Operations, September 1934. This photograph shows dump trucks dropping clay at the head of the road. The clay was laid in a thick bed and graded to form the road surface. (National Park Service Records, National Archives.)

Road Construction, 1934. This view gives an idea of the progress being made on the road construction. Here, the clay road surface is built up on a high subsurface bed of sand as it skirts a low area along the head of the marsh. (Forestry Resources Collection, North Carolina State Archives.)

Prepping the Roadbed for Surfacing. In this photograph, men working ahead of the paving operations are leveling the sandy subsurface roadbed while others in the foreground work to level out the road shoulders. The buildings of the Coast Guard station lie in the distance. (National Park Service Records, National Archives.)

The Completed Road, 1935. This view shows the road as completed in Fort Macon State Park. During its course, the nearly four-mile stretch of road was routed in such a way as to give people views of the ocean and sound as they drove along it. (Fort Macon State Park archives.)

Completion of the Road. This view shows the road as completed outside the town of Atlantic Beach. The road served as a vital link to Fort Macon State Park, although it proved to be treacherous in rainy weather. In 1937, it was finally hard-surfaced with asphalt. (Forestry Resources Collection, North Carolina State Archives.)

Building a Parking Lot. In Fort Macon State Park, the road terminated at a parking lot outside the fort. In this photograph, CCC workers have graded the parking lot and are building a wooden median in its center. Although originally intended for only two or three dozen automobiles, the parking lot has been expanded and lengthened several times over the decades that followed as visitation to the fort increased. (Fort Macon State Park archives.)

Building a Picnic Shelter, 1935. In addition to restoring Fort Macon and completing the road, CCC workers also constructed public facilities for the park. In this photograph, they are building a picnic shelter in a picnic area established near the beach. (National Park Service Records, National Archives.)

Picnic Shelter Completed, 1935. In this photograph, the picnic shelter stands completed. The picnic area was established southwest of the fort near the ocean beach and utilized a road that turned off from the main road through the park. A parking lot and public toilets were also established here. Unfortunately, during 1938–1939, severe shore erosion threatened to wash the facilities away. The picnic shelter was torn down as a result. (National Park Service Records, National Archives.)

BUILDING A HOUSE FOR THE CARETAKER, 1935. Another of the CCC projects was to build a house for a full-time caretaker to look after the park. Here the caretaker's house is up and approaching completion. (National Park Service Records, National Archives.)

CARETAKER'S HOUSE COMPLETED, 1935. This photograph shows the caretaker's house completed. After the fort itself, the house is the second-oldest structure in the park today. (National Park Service Records, National Archives.)

The Nicoll Cottage. North of Fort Macon near the sound was a small former hunting cottage known as the Nicoll Cottage, which became part of Fort Macon State Park when North Carolina acquired the park in 1924. Another CCC project was the renovation of this cottage so that it could be used by the public. (National Park Service Records, National Archives.)

Nicoll Cottage after Renovation, 1935. This photograph shows the completion of the remarkable renovation of the cottage by the CCC. It was to be used as a rental vacation cabin for the park. (National Park Service Records, National Archives.)

Public Latrine Buildings, 1935. The CCC constructed two sets of simple public latrine buildings in Fort Macon State Park. One set was located on the inlet beach east of the fort parking lot, and the other set was located at the park's picnic area southwest of the fort. During 1938–1939, severe shore erosion caused the abandonment of the picnic area. The two latrine buildings there were taken down. (National Park Service Records, National Archives.)

State Park Dock, 1935. Because some visitors to Fort Macon State Park arrived by boat, the CCC built a boat dock on the eastern side of the Coast Guard's boat basin for them to land. This photograph shows the completed dock, with the Nicoll Cottage in the distance. During World War II, however, the dock had to be removed as the Coast Guard expanded its own docking facilities for war use. (National Park Service Records, National Archives.)

Fighting Wind Erosion, 1935. Yet another project of the CCC was to prevent wind erosion from blowing away sand and leaving areas of the park exposed to overwash by the ocean. To combat this erosion, CCC workers formed lines of brush to trap windborne sand and allow the formation of sand dunes. It is a process that is still ongoing in the park today. (National Park Service Records, National Archives.)

Fort Macon Restoration Complete, 1935. As the other projects of road building, erosion control, and the establishment of public park facilities was ongoing, the main focus of CCC work continued to be the restoration of Fort Macon. As this photograph of the casemates beside the northeast stairs shows, the fort was turned into a showcase by the CCC workers. (Fort Macon State Park archives.)

Restored Window Details, 1935. This photograph looking out of the restored window of Casemate 8 reflects the view of what an army officer would have seen in the 1860s and 1870s. The window trim, fanlight window, and inlaid pattern in the plastered window head are reproductions of how the fort appeared in the 1800s. (Fort Macon State Park archives.)

Restored Postern Entrance, 1935. In this view, a CCC worker stands proudly on the restored postern bridge beside a replica of the postern gate. The four-and-a-half-inch-thick gate and its hinges were made by CCC workers. (Fort Macon State Park archives.)

CCC Camp 432 at Fort Macon, April 25, 1935. This photograph shows all of Company 432 of the Civilian Conservation Corps at the height of its work at Fort Macon State Park. Project superintendent Franklin P. Shore sits in the third row left of center, wearing a pith helmet and black tie. Beside him is Capt. E.C. LeGrand, US Army, who oversaw the Army's interests with

the company and assisted with the project. In the background is the Camp Dobbs supply building. The Fort Macon project was completed on October 1, 1935, and Company 432 moved on to other projects. (Fort Macon State Park archives.)

Fort Macon State Park Dedication. On May 1, 1936, Fort Macon State Park was formally dedicated as the first functioning North Carolina state park. Although it was the second state park by acquisition after Mount Mitchell State Park, Fort Macon was the first to be completed and opened as a functioning state park. In this photograph, North Carolina governor J.C.B. Ehringhaus gives the keynote address for the ceremony from the southwest stairs. (Forestry Resources Collection, North Carolina State Archives.)

Park Dedication, May 1, 1936. This is another photograph showing Governor Ehringhaus delivering his address during the dedication of Fort Macon State Park. (Forestry Resources Collection, North Carolina State Archives.)

VIEW THROUGH SALLY PORT ARCHWAY, LATE 1930S. The sight that greeted visitors to Fort Macon State Park as they walked through the sally port in the late 1930s was truly remarkable. Only a few years previous, a tangled jungle of undergrowth and desolation practically hid the fort's walls. This view shows the stark contrast to those seen in the previous chapter. (Fort Macon State Park archives.)

RESTORED EAST FRONT OF THE FORT, C. 1936. This photograph shows the east front of the fort following its restoration and dedication. During the CCC work in the fort, it was the intention of state officials to restore only one half of the fort's casemate fronts to the manner in which they looked in the 1800s. (Fort Macon State Park archives.)

Parade Ground Looking North, c. 1936. This photograph looks across the parade ground toward the sally port entrance. During the CCC restoration of the fort, the casemates on the western half of the fort were left unrestored to provide a contrast to the restored casemates on the opposite side that reflected the fort's appearance in the 1800s. (Fort Macon State Park archives.)

Virginia Barber Humphrey, c. 1940. In 1935, at 61 years old, Lott Williams Humphrey was hired as Fort Macon State Park's first full-time caretaker, a position that would today be considered a park superintendent. His wife, Virginia, assisted with the books, rentals, and payroll. When Lott Humphrey died in March 1939, Virginia was retained as the park caretaker. As such, she was one of the first women in the country to hold such a position. (Fort Macon State Park archives.)

PARK VISITORS ENJOY FORT MACON, C. 1940. This photograph shows park visitors looking out across Fort Macon during the summer of 1939 or 1940. It is one of a number of publicity photographs taken in the park at this time by the North Carolina Department of Conservation and Development. (Fort Macon State Park archives.)

PARK VISITOR ADMIRING THE FORT, C. 1940. Fort Macon State Park's annual visitation fluctuated during the period between 1936 and 1941. The 1936 visitation of 18,534 was the highest for this period, with a low of 9,537 for 1937. Even during 1941, as many men were going into the military and the country was bracing for war, the park's visitation was 17,278. (Fort Macon State Park archives.)

THE FORT BAKE OVEN. A great source of curiosity to park visitors in these prewar years was the fort's ancient bake oven. Located in Casemate 12, this massive brick oven had once baked loaves of bread each day for hundreds of men in the fort's garrisons. Unfortunately, in World War II, the oven was demolished during the Army occupation of the fort. (Fort Macon State Park archives.)

THE ROAD TO THE BEACH DEVELOPMENT, 1940. To the public, the one thing Fort Macon State Park lacked was a public bathing facility on the ocean. In response to public requests, state officials began construction of a beach development for public bathing through the Works Progress Administration (WPA). This photograph shows work in progress on the access road to the development in 1940. (Fort Macon State Park archives.)

CONSTRUCTING THE BEACH DEVELOPMENT ROAD, 1940. This photograph from a different angle shows work continuing on the access road to the beach development. This road turned off the main park road a short distance from the park entrance. (Fort Macon State Park archives.)

PANORAMA OF THE BEACH DEVELOPMENT SITE, 1940. This photograph looks eastward across the area where workmen are preparing the site of the beach development. The access road in the previous two photographs comes in from the left. Because of the severe erosion of the ocean beach in front of the fort, which had caused the loss of the picnic area, the beach development was situated more than a mile from the fort near the park entrance, where there was less chance of erosion. (North Carolina State Archives.)

View of the Bathhouse, 1940. The beach development would feature a bathhouse, concession stand, boardwalk, and parking lot. The bathhouse was set up with a central basket checking area with two attached wings containing men's and women's shower rooms. The bathhouse and other structures were still not quite complete by the following year, when the advent of war diverted the WPA workers to military projects and left the Fort Macon project unfinished. (Fort Macon State Park archives.)

Four

World War II

Soldiers on a Gun Position, 1942. Shortly after the United States entered World War II, troops of the Army Coast Artillery occupied Fort Macon State Park for the war emergency. These soldiers, mostly wearing helmets from the First World War, stand atop an artillery position for a 155-milimeter gun on the beach southwest of the fort. (George H. King Collection, Fort Macon State Park archives.)

Readying Fort Macon for War, c. December 1941. Fort Macon State Park was occupied for war on December 21, 1941, by elements of the 244th Coast Artillery Regiment. Many of the fort casemates were open and provided little comfort from winter elements. Civilian contractors were hired to outfit the casemates with flooring, doors, windows, and electricity as needed. This photograph shows the bustle inside the parade ground as this work is being done. (Harry I. McGinnis Collection, Fort Macon State Park archives.)

Outfitting the Casemates for Troops, c. December 1941. In this photograph, civilian contractors are cutting lumber for flooring and preparing the fort casemates as living quarters for soldiers. (Harry I. McGinnis Collection, Fort Macon State Park archives.)

East Front Casemates, 1942. The casemates of the east front of the parade ground housed the various sections of the headquarters company for the Fort Macon defenses. This photograph shows a bulletin board and a swallowtail guidon, indicating the headquarters for 1st Battalion, 244th Coast Artillery. (Lawrence P. Hansen Collection, Fort Macon State Park archives.)

Snow in Fort Macon, January 6 or 7, 1942. The work to outfit the casemates of the fort with windows, doors, and flooring for the soldiers apparently was completed none too soon. This photograph shows a snow-covered parade ground. On January 6, 1942, two inches of snow fell in the area, which would have made living conditions miserable if the casemates had not been enclosed. (George H. King Collection, Fort Macon State Park archives.)

Soldiers by the Cistern. This photograph shows some of the men of the 244th Coast Artillery in December 1941 or January 1942. They are, from left to right, Sergeants Harry I. McGinnis, Paul C. Hanley, and Anthony F. Lida standing outside Fort Macon. In the background at the right is the old brick cistern. (Harry I. McGinnis Collection, Fort Macon State Park archives.)

Soldiers at the Window of Casemate 24. This view, taken in December 1941, shows, from left to right, soldiers Louis Shuff, Raymond Carey, Joseph Waddle, Charles Kuharich, and Pasquale Parascondola posing in front of Casemate 24. (George H. King Collection, Fort Macon State Park archives.)

Digging in the Guns. Members of the 244th Coast Artillery dig in one of their 155-millimeter guns on the beach near Fort Macon in December 1941. Battery B, 244th Coast Artillery, established an artillery position in the sand dunes southwest of Fort Macon for its four 155-millimeter guns. (George H. King Collection, Fort Macon State Park archives.)

Cannon Drill with a 155-Millimeter Gun, 1942. Soldiers of Battery B, 244th Coast Artillery, hold cannon drill with one of their guns on the beach southwest of Fort Macon. Note the sandbag emplacements that have been created around the guns. (Joseph D. Sebes Collection, Fort Macon State Park archives.)

READY, AIM, FIRE! Soldiers of Battery B, 244th Coast Artillery, hold cannon drill with one of the 155-millimeter guns on the beach southwest of Fort Macon. (Joseph D. Sebes Collection, Fort Macon State Park archives.)

GUN CREW OF A 155-MILLIMETER GUN, 1942. This photograph shows the crew of a 155-millimeter gun preparing to load. Two men in the background are bringing up a shell on a trolley. The structure on top of the sand dune in the rear serves as the battery commander's post with sighting instruments. This structure was later replaced by a concrete bunker with a plotting room. (Joseph D. Sebes Collection, Fort Macon State Park archives.)

The Gun Crew Poses, 1942. In this photograph, the crew of one of the 155-millimeter guns poses behind it. Note the camouflage netting that has been erected over the gun position. (George H. King Collection, Fort Macon State Park archives.)

Soldiers on the Gun Position, 1942. In this photograph, a group of soldiers poses on the gun position of one of the 155-millimeter guns on the beach southwest of Fort Macon. Some of them are posing on the cannon barrel itself. (Joseph D. Sebes Collection, Fort Macon State Park archives.)

THE REAR OF A 155-MILLIMETER GUN, 1942. This photograph shows what the gun crew sees as they load a 155-millimeter gun. Two shells flank a third shell on the loading trolley waiting to be slid into the open breech of the gun. The shells weighed 95 pounds and could be fired more than 10 miles. (John Srutkowski Collection, Fort Macon State Park archives.)

READY AMMUNITION, 1942. Soldier John McMahon sits on palettes of 155-millimeter ready ammunition in the rear of the Battery B gun position southwest of Fort Macon. (George H. King Collection, Fort Macon State Park archives.)

SOLDIERS POSE WITH AMMUNITION, 1942. Soldiers of Battery B, 244th Coast Artillery, pose with 155-millimeter shells in the rear of their battery position. (Joseph D. Sebes Collection, Fort Macon State Park archives.)

5-INCH GUN ON CAPE LOOKOUT, 1942. Officers inspect the crew of a new 5-inch gun in an emplacement on nearby Cape Lookout. In late 1942, the four 155-millimeter guns at Fort Macon of Battery B, 244th Coast Artillery, and two other 155-millimeter guns on Cape Lookout were replaced by pedestal-mounted naval guns on concrete emplacements. A battery of two 5-inch guns was established on Cape Lookout, as seen in this photograph. Another battery of two 6-inch guns was established in the sand dunes at Fort Macon close to Battery B's old site southwest of the fort. (Courtesy of the Casemate Museum, Fort Monroe, Virginia.)

Soldier and Machine Gun, 1943. In this photograph, a soldier mans a water-cooled .50-caliber machine gun, which provided flanking and antiaircraft defense at the battery site. (George H. King Collection, Fort Macon State Park archives.)

Base End Station Tower, 1942. This photograph shows a base end station tower at Fort Macon. These towers were used to take bearings on an offshore target. By triangulating the bearings taken from two or more towers, the target's location and course could be plotted. (George H. King Collection, Fort Macon State Park archives.)

Observer in the Sand Dunes, 1942. In this photograph, Pvt. Herbert K. Pummford uses an observation telescope in the sand dunes in Fort Macon State Park. These telescopes were used for observing enemy targets and directing artillery fire. (Jack M. Garrison Collection, Fort Macon State Park archives.)

Fort Macon Exchange, 1942. During the army occupation of Fort Macon State Park, the park's former vacation cabin, the Nicoll Cottage, was used for a time as the post exchange for the soldiers occupying the fort. Later, an intercept center for mobile radio direction finder stations on Bogue Banks was set up in the cottage to help track the radio transmissions of German U-boat submarines offshore. (George H. King Collection, Fort Macon State Park archives.)

Harbor Entrance Control Post, 1943. In 1942, a Harbor Entrance Control Post (HECP) was established in a signal tower on top of Fort Macon. Joint Army and Navy personnel in this tower were charged with observing shipping movements, identifying all shipping entering Beaufort Inlet, and coordinating Army and Navy harbor defenses. (Thomas McKeon Collection, Fort Macon State Park archives.)

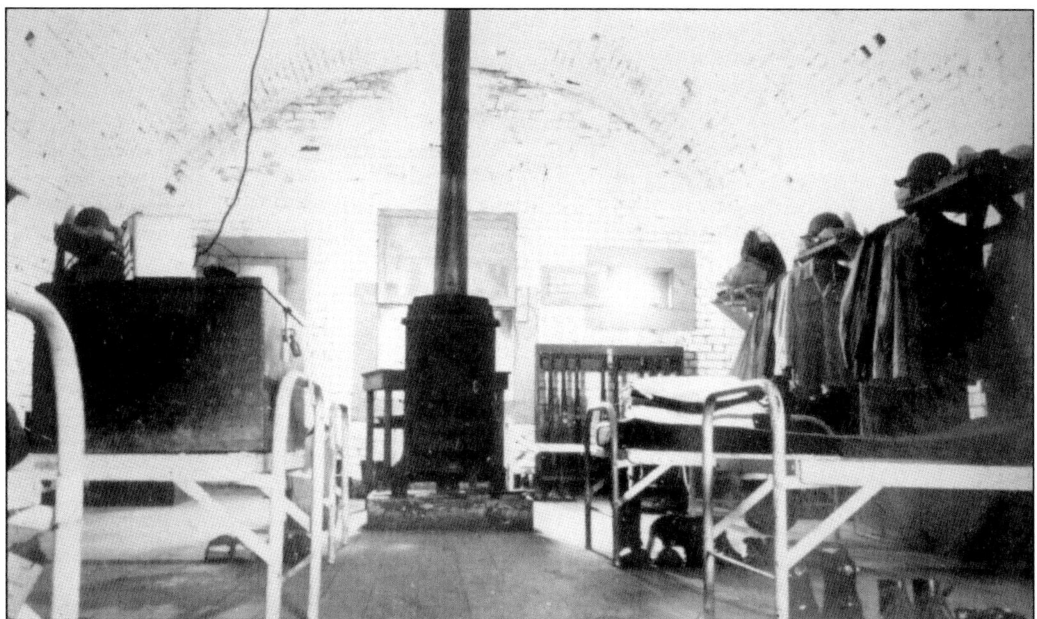

Casemate Interior, 1943. This photograph shows the interior of Casemate 16 in Fort Macon as set up for soldier quarters in 1943. This stands in stark contrast to living conditions of soldiers in the fort during the War Between the States (see page 20), where 20 to 40 men might occupy a single casemate and sleep on four-man wooden bunks. (Thomas McKeon Collection, Fort Macon State Park archives.)

Barracks Area, 1943. In addition to quartering soldiers inside the fort itself, the army constructed a small post outside the fort with barracks for additional soldiers, latrines, a mess hall, recreation building, and workshops. This photograph looks northward from the HECP tower on top of the fort toward the barracks area. (Thomas McKeon Collection, Fort Macon State Park archives.)

Battery Barracks Area, 1943. This photograph shows the barracks area for the soldiers manning the six-inch gun battery in the sand dunes southwest of Fort Macon. Note the camouflage paint on the buildings. (Courtesy Mallory Liles Jr.)

Aerial of Fort Macon, January 1945. This aerial photograph shows the barracks complexes established by the army around Fort Macon in World War II. The buildings in the upper right portion of the photograph are those in the photograph on the previous page. The buildings in the lower left portion are those pictured above. Following the end of the war, all these buildings were removed by the time the Army returned Fort Macon State Park to the State of North Carolina on October 1, 1946. (Fort Macon State Park archives.)

Five

A Modern Park

Picture Perfect. Two ladies are framed through a casemate window as they pose for a photographer in this 1950s publicity photograph for the North Carolina Division of State Parks. With World War II over, Fort Macon State Park resumed its former life as a North Carolina state park. Visitors flocked to the park in ever-increasing numbers, and the park's facilities changed to accommodate them over the decades that followed. (Fort Macon State Park archives.)

Cleanup after World War II. The departure of the Army after the end of the war left a great deal of work to be done to return the park to normal peacetime activities. This 1946 photograph gives an idea of the deplorable condition of the fort following its abandonment by the Army. (Bayard Wootten Photographic Collection, University of North Carolina.)

View through the Sally Port, 1949. After many months of hard work, the fort once again was made to look much like it did before the war. From an estimated annual attendance of 6,000 in 1946, the number of visitors to the park rose to 95,212 in 1949. (Fort Macon State Park archives.)

The Park Bathhouse, c. 1950. Following the war, the park was unable to open its bathhouse facilities to the public until August 1949. This was the first time they had actually been used by the public since their construction eight years earlier. This photograph shows the bathhouse awaiting its first full season in the summer of 1950. (Fort Macon State Park archives.)

Park Concession Stand, 1950. The park concession stand sat at the west end of a wooden boardwalk extending the length of the park's recreation beach. (Fort Macon State Park archives.)

Walkway to the Fort, August 1954. The photographs that follow take an imaginary visitor on a tour of Fort Macon in the 1950s. Here, the walkway leading to the fort from the parking lot passes the old brick cistern standing just outside the fort. (Fort Macon State Park archives.)

Six-Pounder Cannon. Standing just outside the fort was a 6-pounder field cannon placed on display in 1953. The cannon was an original fieldpiece from the War Between the States purchased by the park. The roof of a new rest room building is visible in the background. (Fort Macon State Park archives.)

THE ROADWAY INTO THE FORT, 1956. Visitors walk down the old roadway to the sally port bridge. (Fort Macon State Park archives.)

SALLY PORT ENTRANCE, 1956. This view looks toward the sally port entrance to the fort from the east. Buildings of the adjacent Coast Guard station are visible in the background. (Lewis P. Watson Collection, Fort Macon State Park archives.)

Interior of the Sally Port, 1956. As visitors entered the sally port, they would sign a guest registry at the left. A podium in front of the door held brochures, while a sign at the right listed interesting facts about the fort's history. Because the hinges for the two gates had been stolen by vandals in the early 1900s, the gates were simply propped against the wall. (Fort Macon State Park archives.)

Visitors in the Parade Ground, August 1954. A group of park visitors descends the northeast stairs near the sally port entrance. Under the tree to the left are two 10-inch siege mortars lying on the ground. (Fort Macon State Park archives.)

10-inch Siege Mortars. Originally part of the fort's armament, these two 10-inch siege mortars (minus their gun carriages) were given to the City of Raleigh as monuments in 1902 but were returned to the fort in 1953. Because their gun carriages were long gone, they were simply placed for display on the ground under the trees in the parade ground. (Fort Macon State Park archives.)

Wax Myrtles Framing the Northeast Stairs, 1953. This publicity photograph taken for the North Carolina Division of State Parks shows a view of the northeast stairs through the stand of wax myrtles growing in the parade ground. (Lewis P. Watson Collection, Fort Macon State Park archives.)

View of the Parade Ground through the Trees, 1956. By the 1950s, the old trees left by the CCC in the fort parade ground had grown quite large. They consisted of several cedar trees, a mulberry tree, a stand of large wax myrtles, and a Hercules club or "Toothache Tree." (Fort Macon State Park archives.)

View of the Southwest Stairs, 1953. This is another publicity view of the southwest stairs, framed by the trees. On hot summer days, the trees provided ample shade for park visitors. (Lewis P. Watson Collection, Fort Macon State Park archives.)

Looking across the Parade Ground, 1956. This view looks across the parade ground toward the sally port entrance and the casemates of the east front. (Fort Macon State Park archives.)

Cloud Effect from the Fort Ramparts, 1956. The photograph looks northward across the parade ground from the ramparts with a stunning cloud effect in the background. (Fort Macon State Park archives.)

East Front from the Fort Ramparts, 1953. This publicity view looks from the ramparts toward the casemates of the east front and the southeast stairs. (Lewis P. Watson Collection, Fort Macon State Park archives.)

Southeast Front from the Fort Ramparts, 1953. This publicity view looks across to the southeast front of the parade ground while visitors stroll about. (Lewis P. Watson Collection, Fort Macon State Park archives.)

CHATTING WITH A RANGER, 1956. This photograph shows two park visitors chatting with park superintendent Smith Ray on the ramparts of the fort. The town of Beaufort can be seen in the distant background. (Fort Macon State Park archives.)

AN EXCURSION INTO THE DITCH, 1956. In the ditch, park visitors travel a well-worn trail through the weeds to see the counterfire rooms under the fort's outer wall. The patches of dark bricks along the upper part of the fort's wall denote the places where Union artillery fire struck on April 25, 1862. The damaged wall was repaired after the battle with different-colored bricks. (Fort Macon State Park archives.)

A Couple Relaxing in a Window. This publicity photograph shows a couple relaxing in the window of Casemate 22 in 1951. In 1950, the park's annual attendance stood at 193,364. Since that time, visitation has steadily increased. In 1983, the park's attendance broke the one-million-visitor mark. (Fort Macon State Park archives.)

Window in Casemate 2, 1953. This publicity photograph looks out of the window of Casemate 2 into the parade ground. (Lewis P. Watson Collection, Fort Macon State Park archives.)

Miss North Carolina, 1956. The 1956 Miss North Carolina Pageant was held in Morehead City in July 1956. This publicity photograph shows the newly crowned Miss North Carolina 1956, Joan Spinks Melton of Albemarle, posing in the fort. (Fort Macon State Park archives.)

Miss North Carolina 1956 Posing in Fort Macon. Miss North Carolina 1956 Joan Spinks Melton poses in a window of Fort Macon as photographers and reporters snap her picture. (Fort Macon State Park archives.)

Fort Macon Museum, 1956. During the 1950s, Casemates 2 and 3 were set up with display cases and exhibits about the fort's history. This photograph shows some of the completed displays. (Fort Macon State Park archives.)

Visitors in the Fort Museum. In this view, a family pauses to look at one of the displays in the fort museum. (Fort Macon State Park archives.)

The Bathhouse Area, 1956. The park's bathhouse area saw its first full summer of operations in 1950. Since that time, millions of visitors have enjoyed its opportunities for recreation. This view looks east across the bathhouse parking lot with the bathhouse (center) flanked by the concession stand (right) and a supplemental bathhouse (left). (Fort Macon State Park archives.)

The Park Bathhouse, 1956. By the time this photograph was taken, the bathhouse had changed somewhat from its 1940 appearance. It was enlarged and modernized to meet the park's growing attendance. Damages from hurricanes caused it to be repaired a number of times. (Fort Macon State Park archives.)

A Summer Day at the Bathhouse Area, 1950s. This publicity photograph shows park visitors enjoying a summer day at the bathhouse beach. (Fort Macon State Park archives.)

Lifeguards Stand Watch, 1956. This photograph shows lifeguards keeping watch over park visitors at the bathhouse beach. Lifeguards have been hired by the park to protect swimmers almost every summer since 1949. (Fort Macon State Park archives.)

A Day at the Beach, 1950s. A family group relaxes and enjoys their visit to the Fort Macon beach in this publicity photograph. In addition to providing bathhouse services and lifeguards, the park also rented umbrellas to visitors for a dollar a day. (Fort Macon State Park archives.)

Sun Shelters, 1956. Along the boardwalk on either side of the bathhouse were sun shelters for those visitors who wanted a relaxing day at the beach without exposure to the hot summer sun. (Fort Macon State Park archives.)

Visitors at the Concession Stand, 1956. One of the popular spots at the Fort Macon beach was the little concession stand building, selling all kinds of drinks, ice cream, and food items, as well as cigarettes, cigars, sun tan products, film, aspirin, headache powder, sunglasses, band-aids, and iodine. Note the prices of these items. (Fort Macon State Park archives.)

Visitors at the Bathhouse Window, 1956. This photograph shows visitors purchasing their tickets to use the bathhouse. The bathhouse had 1,000 baskets that could be rented for 25¢ for adults and 16¢ for children. This included shower privileges with soap and towel furnished. Visitors could even rent a swimsuit for 25¢. (Fort Macon State Park archives.)

Picnic Shelter, 1956. Overlooking the west end of the bathhouse parking lot on a large sand dune stood a large picnic shelter. The shelter held 14 picnic tables and offered a panoramic view of the area. (Fort Macon State Park archives.)

Interior of the Picnic Shelter, 1956. This view shows family groups enjoying the picnic shelter. A large barbecue pit stood at the east end of the shelter for visitors to grill their food. (Fort Macon State Park archives.)

Overview of the Bathhouse Parking Lot, 1956. This photograph looks west across the bathhouse parking lot in August 1956. The picnic shelter is visible on the sand dune in the background. The bathhouse and concession stand would be to the left of the photograph out of view. (Fort Macon State Park archives.)

Family Picnics, 1956. This photograph shows families using picnic tables set up on the east side of the bathhouse parking lot in August 1956. Note the metal Coca-Cola and 7-Up coolers. In the 1960s, more picnic tables and shelters were added to this area. (Fort Macon State Park archives.)

FAMILY GROUPS PICNICKING. These publicity photographs were taken of family groups picnicking in 1954 (above) and 1963 (below) at tables provided at the foot of the large picnic shelter. Family picnics, usually on Sunday afternoons, were popular pastimes of the period and made Fort Macon State Park a popular destination in the 1950s and 1960s. (Fort Macon State Park archives.)

Fishing on Bogue Point, 1956. Fishing has always been another important recreational opportunity of Fort Macon State Park. In this photograph, anglers take advantage of the numerous stone jetties along both Bogue Point and the ocean beach to try their hand at catching fish. (Fort Macon State Park archives.)

Fishing at One of the Jetties, 1956. With storm clouds towering just offshore, fishermen get in a few more casts at one of the stone jetties on the ocean beach built by Army engineers in the 1800s to prevent shore erosion. (Fort Macon State Park archives.)

Gun Emplacements in the Surf, 1950s. Unfortunately, the 1950s and 1960s saw considerable damage done to the park by shore erosion and storms. This photograph shows the concrete gun emplacements for two World War II six-inch Navy guns lying in the surf after shore erosion undermined them. These emplacements had stood some distance from the sea when they were built less than 10 years earlier. (Fort Macon State Park archives.)

Aerial View of Fort Macon, c. 1959. In this photograph, many of the trees that had been in the fort's parade ground for years are gone. They were destroyed by Hurricane Helene in September 1958. The remaining trees would all be destroyed the following year by Hurricane Donna. (Fort Macon State Park archives.)

HURRICANE DONNA DAMAGE. This photograph shows the boardwalk at the bathhouse area demolished by Hurricane Donna in September 1960. Donna did severe damage throughout the park, destroying the boardwalk and sun shelters at the bathhouse and eroding away the beach and barrier sand dunes. (Fort Macon State Park archives.)

SEA JETTY CONSTRUCTION, 1961. As a result of the severe erosion taking place in the park, a joint state/federal project was initiated in 1961 to construct a seawall/sea jetty structure to stop the loss of beach. This photograph, taken in December 1961, shows construction well underway. The structure was not finished until 1970 but ultimately proved successful in stopping the erosion. (Fort Macon State Park archives.)

DESTRUCTION OF THE BATHHOUSE. A storm in December 1967 undermined the old 1940 bathhouse that had served park visitors for so many years. A portion of the bathhouse collapsed, but part of it continued in use for one more summer until a new bathhouse was built. (Fort Macon State Park archives.)

A NEW BATHHOUSE FOR THE PARK. In 1969, this new bathhouse was completed for the park, replacing the ruined 1940 bathhouse. Although it was subsequently destroyed by fire in 1978, it was replaced by another bathhouse of a similar design that still exists today. (Fort Macon State Park archives.)

MODERN AERIAL OF BOGUE POINT. This modern aerial photograph facing northwest shows Bogue Point as it appeared in May 2003. Fort Macon is in the foreground, and the town of Morehead City is in the background. The town of Atlantic Beach appears in the left distance, and the US Coast Guard base is on the far side of the fort. Note the amount of beach that has built up behind the sea jetty over the years. (Diane Hardy Collection, Fort Macon State Park archives.)

Modern View of Fort Macon and Visitor Center, 2012. This photograph shows how Fort Macon looks today. A major addition to the park was a new education and visitor center (background), which was completed in 2009. Between the times when attendance records started being kept in 1930 and the year 2000, almost 26 million visitors have visited Fort Macon State Park. Today, its annual visitation hovers around one and a quarter million visitors, making this beloved park one of the most visited in the North Carolina state park system. (Courtesy Jody A. Merritt, former superintendent of Fort Macon State Park.)

Consistent with our mission to preserve history on a local level, this book was printed in South Carolina on American-made paper and manufactured entirely in the United States. Products carrying the accredited Forest Stewardship Council (FSC) label are printed on 100 percent FSC-certified paper.